T0014682

REDESIGNING CITIES
TO FIGHT CLIMATE CHANGE
by Cynthia Kennedy Henzel

FOCUS
READERS.

NAVIGATOR

WWW.FOCUSREADERS.COM

Focus Readers is distributed by North Star Editions:
sales@northstareditions.com | 888-417-0195

Produced for Focus Readers by Red Line Editorial.

Content Consultant: Jeremy S. Hoffman, PhD, David and Jane Cohn Scientist, Science Museum of Virginia

Photographs ©: Shutterstock Images, cover, 1, 4–5, 7, 8–9, 13, 14–15, 17, 21, 22–23, 25, 27, 29; Red Line Editorial, 11; Masanori Inagaki/Yomiuri Shimbun/AP Images, 18

Library of Congress Cataloging-in-Publication Data
Names: Henzel, Cynthia Kennedy, 1954- author.
Title: Redesigning cities to fight climate change / by Cynthia Kennedy Henzel.
Description: Lake Elmo, MN : Focus Readers, [2023] | Series: Fighting climate change with science | Includes index. | Audience: Grades 4-6
Identifiers: LCCN 2022007151 (print) | LCCN 2022007152 (ebook) | ISBN 9781637392744 (hardcover) | ISBN 9781637393260 (paperback) | ISBN 9781637394250 (pdf) | ISBN 9781637393789 (ebook)
Subjects: LCSH: City planning--Climatic factors--Juvenile literature. | Climate change mitigation--Juvenile literature. | Renewable energy sources--Juvenile literature. | Sustainable urban development--Juvenile literature.
Classification: LCC TD168.5 .H46 2023 (print) | LCC TD168.5 (ebook) | DDC 307.1/216--dc23/eng/20220303
LC record available at https://lccn.loc.gov/2022007151
LC ebook record available at https://lccn.loc.gov/2022007152

Printed in the United States of America
Mankato, MN
082022

ABOUT THE AUTHOR

Cynthia Kennedy Henzel has a BS in social studies education and an MS in geography. She has worked as a teacher-educator in many countries. Currently, she writes fiction and nonfiction books and develops education materials for social studies, history, science, and ELL students. She has written more than 100 books and more than 150 stories for young people.

TABLE OF CONTENTS

CHAPTER 1

A TALE OF TWO STORMS

In 2005, Hurricane Katrina hit the US Gulf Coast. In New Orleans, Louisiana, many of the city's **levees** failed. As a result, most of the city flooded. People had to leave. The flooding harmed low-income people and Black people the most. These communities also received the least amount of government help.

In 2005, Hurricane Katrina forced approximately 1.5 million people out of their homes.

Katrina was one of the strongest storms in US history. But **climate change** was making strong storms more common. So, the US government worked to protect New Orleans. Workers built new levees.

The new levees' first test came in 2021. Scientists warned people about Hurricane Ida. Many people left for safer areas. But others could not afford to leave.

Hurricane Ida hit New Orleans on August 29. Thankfully, the city's new levees worked. Some areas flooded. But the flooding was much less harmful than it had been during Hurricane Katrina.

However, Ida caused other damage. Strong winds toppled weak power lines.

Hurricane Katrina's deaths were largely due to flooding. Ida's deaths were mostly from the heat and lack of power.

As a result, the city's **electrical grid** collapsed. Most of New Orleans lost power for days. The city was facing extreme heat, and people did not have air-conditioning. Hurricane Ida had shown just how much cities needed to adapt to climate change.

CHAPTER 2

CLIMATE CHANGE AND CITIES

People are causing the climate crisis. They mainly do so by burning **fossil fuels**. Using these fuels releases carbon dioxide (CO_2) into the air. CO_2 traps heat. That heat is leading to climate change.

In some ways, cities help limit climate change. That's because cities pack more people into smaller spaces. Then, the

Cities use 78 percent of the world's energy. But they tend to produce less carbon dioxide per person than rural and suburban areas.

same amount of energy can reach more people. As a result, cities tend to produce less CO_2 per person than rural areas do.

Even so, cities are contributing to climate change. Transportation is one major source. Many people drive cars in cities. Gasoline powers most of these cars. Burning gasoline releases CO_2.

Sprawl around cities makes this problem worse. Suburbs surround many US cities. These areas are very spread out. And many are designed around cars. So, people must drive much more in suburbs. That burns even more gasoline.

City buildings are another large user of fossil fuels. These buildings are often made of concrete and steel. Producing these materials releases lots of CO_2. It takes energy to heat and cool buildings, too. Buildings also use large amounts of electricity. Fossil-fuel power plants provide most of that electricity.

URBAN SPRAWL

Atlanta, Georgia, and Barcelona, Spain, have similar populations. But Atlanta's sprawl means it produces much more CO_2 per person from transportation.

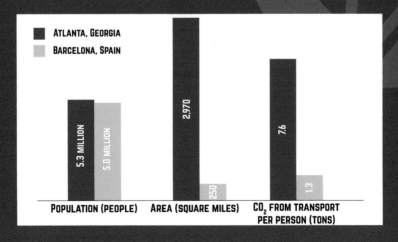

ATLANTA, GEORGIA
BARCELONA, SPAIN

5.3 MILLION
5.0 MILLION
2,970
250
7.6
1.3

POPULATION (PEOPLE)   AREA (SQUARE MILES) CO_2 FROM TRANSPORT PER PERSON (TONS)

Cities are especially affected by climate change. For instance, most large cities are near the ocean. And climate change is causing ocean levels to rise. As a result, coastal cities are at more risk of flooding.

Climate risks are not spread equally in cities. Low-income areas tend to have

HIDDEN CO$_2$

Buying products adds CO_2 to the air. But it can be hard to recognize. For example, talking on a phone doesn't add CO_2. But a company mined metals for the phone. Ships and trucks moved all these materials to the factory that made the phone. They also brought the phone to a store. Finally, charging a phone uses electricity. Each step produces CO_2.

Cities are covered with streets and parking lots, so water can't soak into the ground. That's why cities flood easily.

worse **infrastructure**. This infrastructure cannot withstand extreme weather as well. Low-income people also have fewer resources. So, they might not be able to afford leaving before a disaster. And they might not be able to rebuild after one.

CHAPTER 3

BUILDING BETTER CITIES

Redesigning cities can slow the climate crisis. Buildings are one key place to focus. They can use less steel and concrete. Design matters, too. For instance, skyscrapers are often built close together. These buildings trap heat. This type of extra urban heat is called the heat island effect. As a result, city buildings

Cities that build upward can increase the urban heat island effect unless they also make more trees and green spaces.

need more energy to stay cool. Using that energy releases CO_2.

Cities can also work on **electrification**. For example, cities can remove natural gas furnaces in buildings. Electric heating can replace furnaces. Electricity is more **efficient** than fossil fuels. So, less energy overall can meet the same needs.

Renewable energy can also be the source of electricity. Unlike fossil fuels, renewable energy does not run out. It also does not produce CO_2 during use. Examples of renewable energy include wind power and solar power.

Cities can change transportation as well. They can reduce the amount of

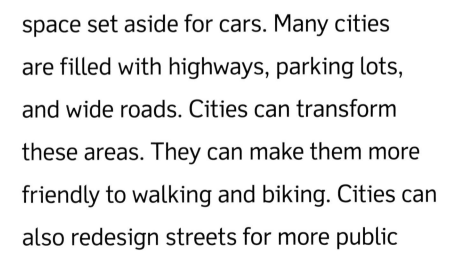

Some cities were never built for cars. In Venice, Italy, people travel by boat.

space set aside for cars. Many cities are filled with highways, parking lots, and wide roads. Cities can transform these areas. They can make them more friendly to walking and biking. Cities can also redesign streets for more public

Rooftop gardens in cities help control temperature, energy use, and pollution.

transit. Then, they can add more buses and trains. Public transit is far more efficient than cars. Cities can also replace gasoline-powered public buses and trains with electric ones.

In addition, smart technology can help cities adapt to the climate crisis. Cities can use monitors to collect data. For example, monitors can be installed in storm drains. The monitors alert workers when the drains are clogged. Then workers can clear those drains. That can help prevent flooding during storms.

CATCH THE E-BUS

Santiago, Chile, is home to millions of people. Thousands of buses take residents around the city. In 2018, the city made a huge change. It started buying electric buses. By 2021, hundreds of e-buses were up and running. But Santiago wasn't done. The city planned to electrify all of its buses by 2035.

GROW A HOME

People build cities with wood, concrete, and steel. These materials contribute to climate change. Forests are cut down to obtain wood. People use energy to mine for the raw materials that form concrete and steel. Then, they use more energy to make the raw materials into concrete and steel. Also, buildings made of these materials must be repaired or replaced over time.

Scientists are inventing new building materials that are alive. The new materials are made from living things such as fungi. Examples of fungi include mushrooms, mold, and yeast. The roots of fungi grow into different shapes. They are good insulation for houses. They are not toxic. They do not burn easily. Plus, they are stronger than concrete.

Mushrooms form networks of fiber underground. The fiber is called mycelium. It could be used for building.

These new materials repair themselves. They change as the climate changes. People may someday grow their homes instead of building them!

CHAPTER 4

CHALLENGES AHEAD

Redesigning cities has a variety of challenges. The technology is mostly ready. But scientists are still making improvements. For example, electric buses need powerful batteries. In the early 2020s, e-bus batteries didn't always perform well enough. Even so, batteries were getting better every year.

Electric buses are expensive for cities to buy and use. But scientists and companies are working to reduce the cost.

The climate crisis is already serious. So, changes in cities must take place quickly. But quick changes can be difficult. That's because cities are complex. For example, roads help transport people to home and work. Buses take students to schools. Pipes send clean water to residents. Sewers get rid of dirty water. As a result, even small changes can affect many people.

Large shifts can be politically difficult. Wealthy, white communities often oppose neighborhood change. Cities also need support from state and national governments. And states might not want to pay for changes that cities want.

Decisions made by local and national governments can help or hurt the fight against climate change.

Many different groups keep cities running. For example, some companies provide energy to cities. Other companies construct new buildings. Meanwhile, lawmakers work for residents' interests. Groups must work together. But they often want different things. Some even stop changes. For instance, natural gas companies often oppose electrification. That's because they make money when buildings use gas for heating.

Even so, many cities are pushing ahead. For example, several cities have banned cars. Instead, many people walk or bike. Others take public transit. These bans

FOOD FOR CITIES

Abu Dhabi, United Arab Emirates, is growing food using hydroponics. Hydroponics grows food in water instead of in soil. Vegetables grow indoors in trays of water. The water contains food for the plants. This system saves water. The trays are stacked, which saves space. Food is grown near where it is used. This decreases transportation pollution.

In Bogotá, Colombia, cars are banned every Sunday along certain roads.

lowered air pollution. People's health improved. Plus, cities produced less CO_2.

Another challenge is that all cities are different. Their climate risks are unique. Their solutions vary, too. For instance, Mexico's east coast faces strong storms. Flooding affects the coastal cities. **Coral reefs** help stop the floods. But climate change is killing the reefs. As a result, Mexico's cities are losing natural storm protection. In response, scientists are working to save the reefs. That way, they can also prevent serious flooding.

Strong storms can also cause flooding in New York City. But corals can't survive that far north. So, in 2014, the city tried a new idea. It began growing oysters off the shore. Oysters also form reefs. Like corals, they can act as a storm wall and help prevent flooding.

Fighting the climate crisis in cities is a big task. But joining the effort can be rewarding. In fact, some cities have growing numbers of citizen scientists.

Citizen scientists don't have scientific jobs. But they do help study the world around them. They look for ways to make their cities better.

HOW REEFS STOP FLOODS

Healthy coral reefs absorb wave energy. So, reefs can stop waves from causing floods when they hit shore.

WAVES WITH CORAL REEFS

WAVES WITHOUT CORAL REEFS

FOCUS ON
REDESIGNING CITIES

Write your answers on a separate piece of paper.

1. Write a paragraph describing the main ideas of Chapter 3.

2. What changes do you think are most important for redesigning cities in your area? Why?

3. Flooding from Hurricane Katrina mostly harmed which groups of people?

    A. low-income people and Black people

    B. middle-income people and white people

    C. high-income people and Latino people

4. What is an example of electrification?

    A. changing from gasoline-powered buses to e-buses

    B. using steel in buildings instead of wood

    C. supporting coral reefs to stop flooding

Answer key on page 32.

GLOSSARY

climate change
A human-caused global crisis involving long-term changes in Earth's temperature and weather patterns.

coral reefs
Systems of animals that live in warm, shallow waters.

efficient
Accomplishing as much as possible with as little effort or as few resources as possible.

electrical grid
A complex network that delivers electricity from power sources to users.

electrification
The process of shifting systems to depend on electricity.

fossil fuels
Energy sources that come from the remains of plants and animals that died long ago.

infrastructure
The systems, such as roads, water supplies, and energy distribution, that a city needs to function.

levees
Walls built from earthen materials to stop floodwaters.

TO LEARN MORE

BOOKS

Farrell, Courtney. *Making a City Sustainable*. Minneapolis: Abdo Publishing, 2019.

Heitkamp, Kristina Lyn. *Electric Vehicles*. Lake Elmo, MN: Focus Readers, 2022.

Kurtz, Kevin. *The Future of Cities*. Minneapolis: Lerner Publications, 2021.

NOTE TO EDUCATORS

Visit **www.focusreaders.com** to find lesson plans, activities, links, and other resources related to this title.

INDEX